Requirement	Genre	Tally
	Traditional Literature	
	Realistic Fiction	
	Historical Fiction	
	Fantasy	
	Science Fiction	
	Informational	
	Biography	
	Choice	

Genres at a Glance

Fiction		
Code	**Genre**	**Definition**
TL	Traditional Literature	Stories that are passed down orally from one group to another in history. This includes folktales, fairy tales, fables, legends, and myths from different cultures.
F	Fantasy	Made-up stories that have some elements that could not be true or could not happen in this world (e.g., fairies, talking animals).
SF	Science Fiction	A type of fantasy that uses science and technology (e.g., robots, time machines).
RF	Realistic Fiction	Stories that can be true to life but are mostly from the author's imagination.
HF	Historical Fiction	Stories that take place in the past and are from the author's imagination. They have some truth in them.

Nonfiction		
Code	**Genre**	**Definition**
I	Informational	Texts that provide factual information to readers.
B	Biography	The author tells the story of a real person's life.
AB	Autobiography	The person tells the story of his/her own life.
M	Memoir	The author tells about an experience or a part of his or her life.

© 2002 by I.C. Fountas and G. S. Pinnell, *Reader's Notebook*, NH: Heinemann

Reading List

Select a book to read. Enter the title and author on your reading list. When you have completed it, write the genre and the date. If you have abandoned it, write an (**A**) and the date you abandoned it in the date column. Note whether the book was easy (**E**), just right (**JR**), or a challenging (**C**) book for you.

#	Title	Author	Genre Code	Date Completed	E, JR, C

#	Title	Author	Genre Code	Date Completed	E, JR, C

#	Title	Author	Genre Code	Date Completed	E, JR, C

#	Title	Author	Genre Code	Date Completed	E, JR, C

#	Title	Author	Genre Code	Date Completed	E, JR, C

#	Title	Author	Genre Code	Date Completed	E, JR, C

#	Title	Author	Genre Code	Date Completed	E, JR, C

#	Title	Author	Genre Code	Date Completed	E, JR, C

Topics That Interest Me	Kinds of Books That Interest Me	Authors That Interest Me

Books to Read

Title	Author	Check When Completed

Books to Read

Title	Author	Check When Completed

Title	Author	Check When Completed

Title	Author	Check When Completed

Title	Author	Check When Completed

Title	Author	Check When Completed

Title	Author	Check When Completed

Title	Author	Check When Completed

Title	Author	Check When Completed

Date

Greeting,

Paragraph 1

Paragraph 2

Body

Paragraph 3

Closing,

Signature

Guidelines for Proofreading Your Letter

1. Reread your letter to be sure it makes sense.

2. Be sure you have responded to what the teacher or a peer wrote to you.

3. Write the date.

4. Check the greeting and closing.

5. Check your spelling, capitalization, and punctuation.

Date

Dear _____,

       This year, you and I will write letters to each other about books, reading, writers, and writing. Our letters will give us a chance to share our thoughts and feelings about books.

       Write a letter to me to share your thinking about the book you are reading. The completed letter is due on the day indicated on the Reader's Notebook list. Use the letter format included in this notebook, and be sure to include the title and author of your book, and to underline the title in your letter. It is important that your letters are neat and easy to read so that your thoughts can be easily understood. When you think you have finished, use the proofreading list included in this notebook to check your letter and make sure it is just the way you want it.

       I look forward to reading about your thinking and having interesting conversations with you about books this year.

                                 Eager to read your letter,

Possible Topics for Your Letters

Share your thinking about:

◆ something that surprised you or that you found interesting
◆ what you like or dislike about the book and why
◆ an interesting or important character
◆ parts of the book that puzzled you or made you ask questions
◆ what the story means to you
◆ your thoughts and feelings about the author's message
◆ what you noticed about the characters, such as what made them act as they did or how they changed
◆ why you think the author chose the title
◆ your predictions and whether they were right
◆ how the information in the book fits with what you already know
◆ how the book reminds you of yourself, or people you know or of something that happened in your life
◆ how the book is like other books by the same author, on the same topic, or in the same genre
◆ how the book reminds you of other books, especially the characters, events, or setting
◆ how the illustrations add meaning to the story
◆ the ending and your feelings about it
◆ the language the author used and what you thought about it
◆ the author's craft—what was good about the author's writing
◆ why you chose the book
◆ why you think the author wrote the book
◆ whether or not you would recommend the book to another reader and why
◆ what you would change about the book
◆ examples of stereotypes or biases
◆ whether the book is easy, just right, or challenging for you and how you know

continued on following page

- ◆ the genre and its characteristics
- ◆ the author's use of time in the story
- ◆ how the setting affects the characters
- ◆ how the author captured your interest or pulled you into the book
- ◆ how the author builds suspense
- ◆ what you want to remember about this book
- ◆ new insights or understandings you have
- ◆ why you abandoned the book

Ways to Have a Good Discussion

Read and think about...

◆ what you find interesting or surprising

◆ how the author makes you feel

◆ what you like/dislike about the writing

◆ what the author is trying to say and how you feel about it

◆ what the book makes you think

◆ your reaction to the characters

◆ how the book reminds you of your life

◆ how the book reminds you of other books

◆ how the book is similar to or different from other books by this author or other books in this genre

◆ what you don't understand, find confusing, or have questions about

◆ what you notice about the illustrations

◆ what you want to remember about the book

◆ places where the author gives good descriptions

◆ why you think the author wrote the book

◆ what the author is really trying to say

◆ what you notice about the author's craft

◆ how the author used time

◆ examples of stereotypes or other biases

◆ what you notice about the author's language, word choice, or style

◆ what you learned

© 2002 by I.C. Fountas and G. S. Pinnell, *Reader's Notebook*, NH: Heinemann

1. Be prepared.

2. Sit so everyone can see everyone else.

3. Get started right away.

4. Look at the person who is talking.

5. Listen to understand.

6. Ask questions to understand better.

7. Speak clearly but not too loudly.

8. Wait for the speaker to finish.

9. Use language that invites the opinions of others.

10. Be sure everyone gets a turn.

11. Build on one another's ideas.

12. Respect one another's ideas.

13. Stay on the topic.

14. Provide evidence from your experience or from the text to support your thinking.